The Edge of Hope

The moments that almost broke me
& Other musings

the edge of hope

robin williams

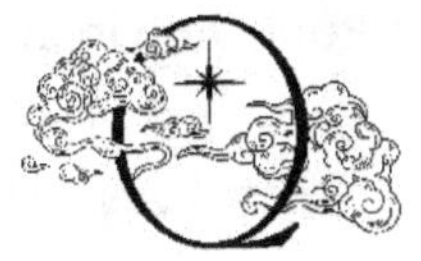

Q an Imprint of Querencia Press
Chicago, IL

Q AN IMPRINT OF QUERENCIA PRESS

ISBN 978 1 959118 30 5

www.querenciapress.com

First Published in 2023

**Querencia Press, LLC
Chicago IL**

Printed & Bound in the United States of America

Trigger Warning

The topics in this book are heavy. Be mindful of your health if any
of these trigger you:

Grief
Death
Sexual Assault
Homophobia
Depression
Body Insecurity

Remember to take care of yourselves.

An apology letter pt. 1

Dear ******,

You had my heart at the first hello.
I know it's cliché, but it's true.

The soft gravel of your voice, your arms waving above your head, the pounding of your feet on the wooden bridge holding you above the first of three rivers. I tunneled onto you, your eyes that matched the sky, and that smile, that damned smile. The corner of your lips raised, always half smirking and contagious, my favorite part of you. It's what I remember most when I think of the years we shared together. That and

the hurt. The phone calls on a pink carpet in my uncle's room that I borrowed right after coming back from the mental hospital. The crack in our voices as we talked about what-ifs, as we talked about breaking up, as we talked about me needing to feel certain in my sexuality. The late-night texts, blue light illuminating my bedroom, my sister telling me to get off, to sleep on it, to not let my impulsive pettiness end what we had.

I constantly remind myself that the breakup was mutual, that there was no one to blame, but I know my faults tore apart everything we had. I live inside of my own head so much that I lose the fact of reality, I can't take these words back, I can't apologize and pretend it will be fine forever. God, you loved me so much, but I needed that high of someone caring about losing me, my selfishness to matter, to mean something to someone, that even with it right in front of me, I never saw it. And god, I loved you too, more than anything or anyone I've ever loved before.

————————

Robin Williams

I'm sorry we didn't keep the promises of forever that we made to each other,
but maybe it's better this way.

Best,
Robin

Texts That I Will Never Send pt. 1

1. I wish you would have told me you didn't love me sooner. I wish this would hurt less. Does this hurt you still, too?
2. In truth, I never think about you. I list my past relationships and you are an afterthought, a part of the pain I no longer remember, a moment I will no longer waste my time on.
3. I'm still in love with you.
4. We were stupid teenagers who called something love when it wasn't. I was a stupid teenager who called something love when it wasn't.
5. I sometimes wonder where I would be now if I didn't give you another chance. I think I'd be happier.
6. I'm still pissed you never cared. I'm still pissed that I still do.
7. I think I'll always be in love with you.

And still
She is all I think about,
The what ifs that linger in the air.

Like drops of water having already fallen,
Waiting for the sun to pull them back up into the clouds.
And the ones that never make it back up,
Endlessly churning miles away from land.

Uncertain where fate will take them, leave them
Uncertain where fate will take us, leave me

What if I never rise after this fall?
What if I'm forever floating in an endless ocean?

What if she
Is all I think about
Always?

————⊳◯⊂·⊃◯⊲————

Robin Williams

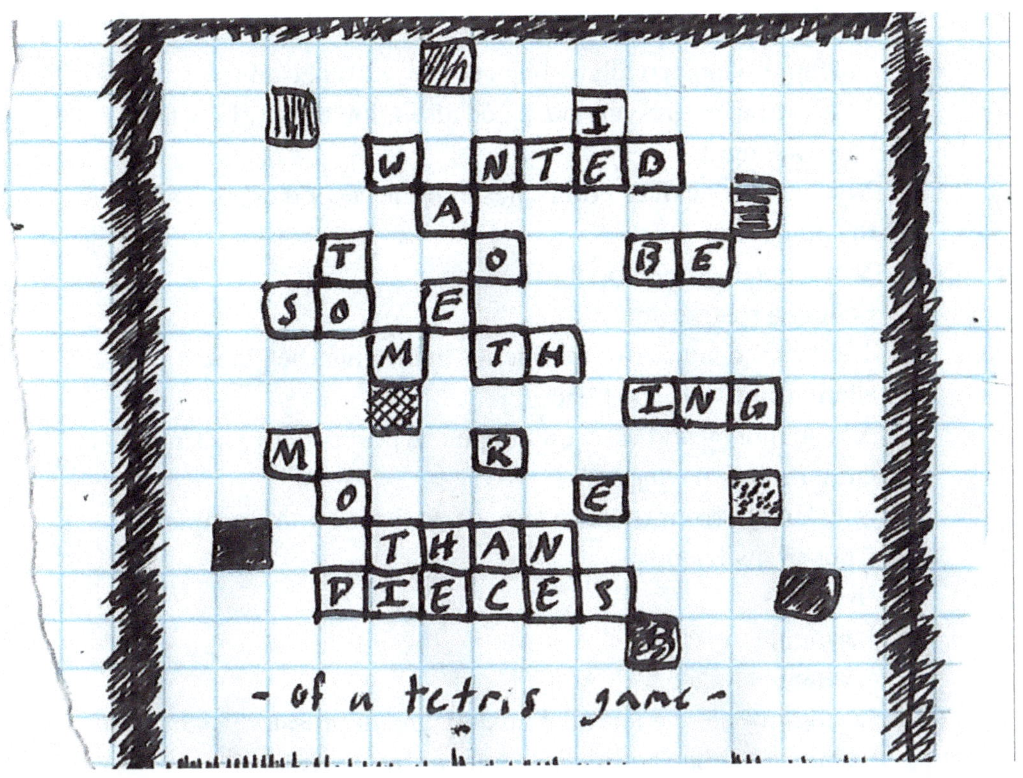
I
WANTED
A
T O BE
S O E
O M TH
M R ING
O E
THAN
PIECES
- of a tetris game -

Things that terrify me, and more:
after Shreya

1. Losing my job because I'm queer.
2. Taking too long to fill my bags at the self-checkout.
3. My hair never growing back because I don't know how to stop pulling it.
4. My friends deciding I don't deserve the second chance and dropping me.
5. Making a doctor's appointment.
6. Calling a restaurant.
8. The DMV, despite my confidence in driving, the place is too silent, too white, too lifeless.
9. All the money and time and hope I've put into my writing career never paying off.
10. Speaking in front of large crowds, in front of new people, in front of my friends.
11. Dying.
12. Losing all my cats.
13. Losing my sister.
14. Losing myself in a spiral of anxiety and depression, taking a trillion steps backwards into unhealthy obsessions.

I don't want to talk about the end of the universe. Let's try small talk instead.

———————•———❯❮❯·❯❮❯———•———

Robin Williams

//They took me to a room with a small table, a block or two,
and a little stuffed toy for the children.
It was all light wood and grey,
a bright palette for all the dark discussions it held.
She sat me down, a woman I only met a few minutes ago,
and asked me.
      Can you tell me what happened? Who did it and where?

I remember reading a book
where they asked the girl the same questions.
She drew a picture of a person
and circled the places where he touched her.
There was paper in front of me,
and I was already fidgeting with a pencil between my fingers.

I drew a person.
Circled the places.
And showed her.

She looked down at the drawing, and then back up to me.
      Can you say these places? Do you know what they're
called?
Of course I knew. What a dumb question to ask me.
But I knew I'd have to get the lump out of my throat.
In the corner was a little recorder.
On the other side of the wall,
the officer and Tinkerbell sat listening.
They needed me to say it.
and I did.

She looked pleased.
I'd forgotten how to breathe.
She asked

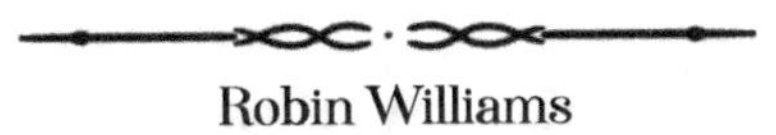

Robin Williams

Can you tell me who and when?

I remember reading a book
where a girl walked home from a party, barefoot, drunk.
So I said that.
She asked
        Where was the party?
I said the street by my house.

the truth is,
that was a lie.
and they'd soon come to know that.

The days went by and I ignored every phone call from the officer.
I went to school with my sister and sat down in the counselor's
room.
My two favorite people, sitting in front of me,
not sure what kind of bomb we were going to drop.
And we told them we were taking our brother to court,
because he assaulted us.
They asked
        Are you okay?
Did we say yes?

We told them I had something important to share.
I had lied.

I told them I made up a boy, made up a story,
made it up so well that I had convinced myself.
I told them I lied because I was scared.
and I was hurt, and feeling guilty,
and wanted no more harm to come to my brother.

Robin Williams

I told them I blamed an imaginary person
for the crimes committed against me
and I wasn't sure how to take it back.
They said
       It's okay, you had every right to be afraid.

The officer called again and I answered.
Sat on my bed with my head in my sister's lap.
He asked me
       Can you tell me their location?

I said my head.
I made him up.
I had thought that if I put the crimes
on somebody you could never find,
my brother wouldn't go to jail.
He said
       Okay.
He hung up.

I still blame the
blond hair blue eyed white boy
with steel toe boots for ruining my life.
maybe because the
black hair green eyed white boy
with his mother's eyebrows, looked too much like me.

I shaved my head once.
Looked in the mirror.
And saw him staring back at me.//

⚬⚬⚬

Robin Williams

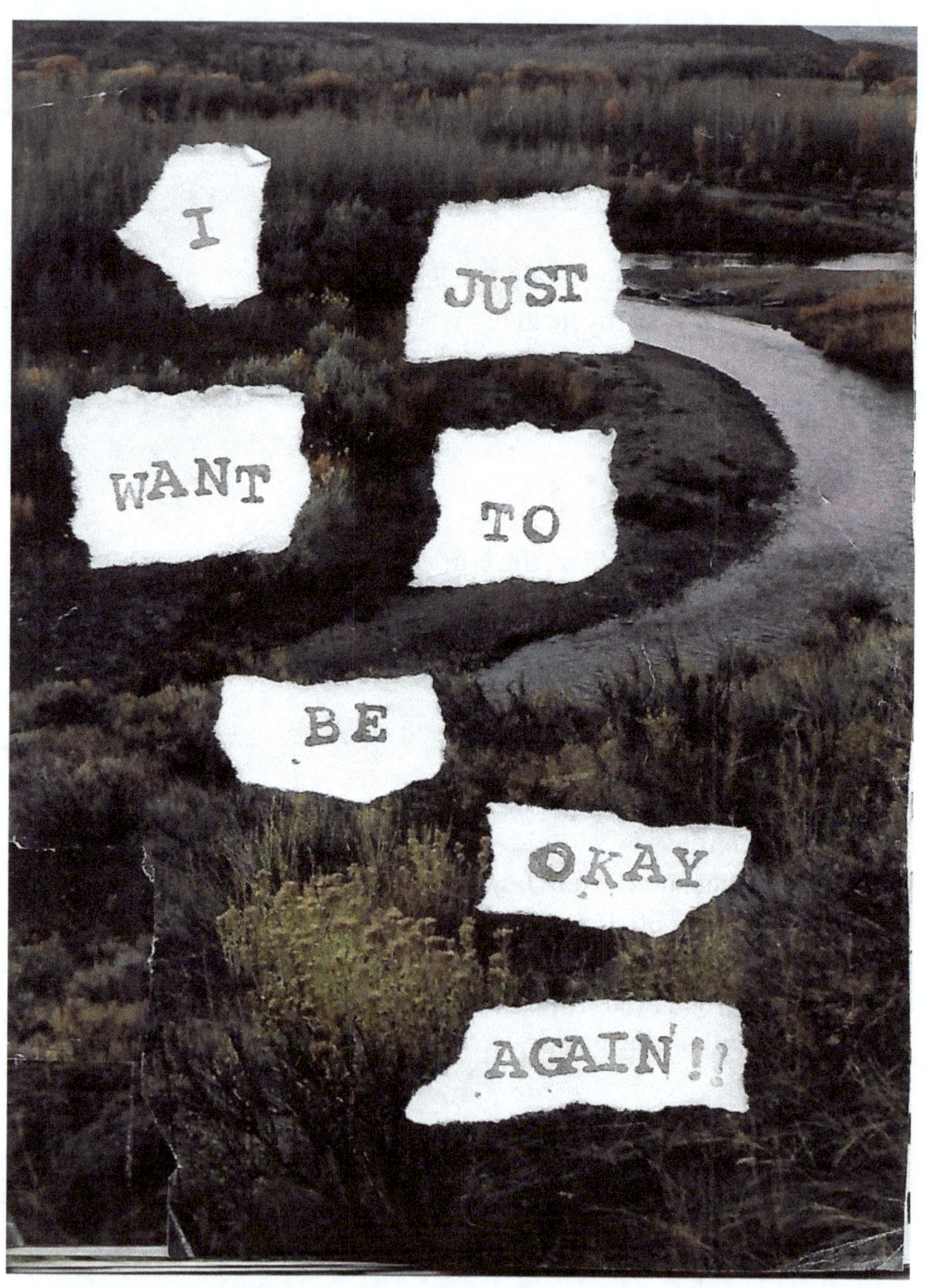

Robin Williams

To The Girl Whose Soul Has Been Taken Back To Mexico//To The Girl Who Was My Friend//To Myra//

It's been two years since you've been gone.
That orange shirt used to be my favorite,
I can't even hold it between my fingers
without thinking of you.

My hands shake every time
I try to stay steady for a winged eyeliner.
The mascara smudges,
black ash on my face.
You were cremated.

I remember driving around on clear days
looking at the sunbeams shining through the clouds.
Everyone said they were the stairways to heaven.

I took pictures that evening in the golden-hour sky,
and I keep looking back behind me,
wondering if you were already standing there.

Robin Williams

What is the time for you?
Is it morning there? Is the sun awake with you?

I ask
but I already know.

I know you are up before the sky even opens its eyes,
the kettle already whistling before the birds first song.

I know you have that worn leather journal your grandfather gave
you cracked open,
scribbling notes and to-do lists on the last of its pages.

I know you will forget them, after your third cup of coffee and
tea now gone cold,
you will forget all the things you had to do just like you will
forget me.

But I couldn't forget you.
No, I don't think I could.

Robin Williams

Loving someone
Only when the
Night falls and the lights
Go off, isn't loving someone.

Did you think
It was?
Someone loving someone
Takes more than
A single call a month.
Needs more than a whisper
Cooing out of fear of love
Ending and fading.

—we could have survived
the distance
if only you'd have tried.

Robin Williams

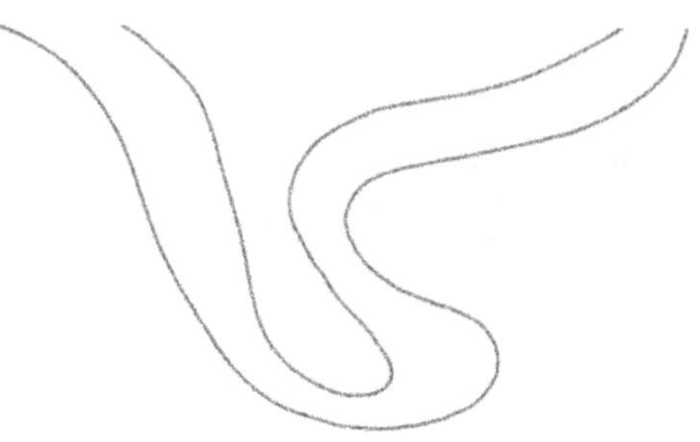

I'M REACHING FOR A LONGING
AND I CANNOT GRASP IT

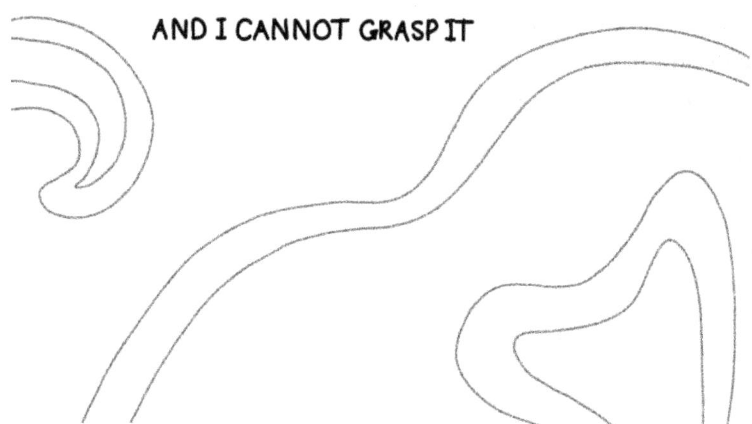

Robin Williams

OUR-RELATIONSHIP WAS
drift·wood
/'drif(t)woŏd/

Noun

1. ~~pieces of wood which are floating on the sea or have been washed ashore.~~
1. We sat on the edge of both stone and wave.
    > When I was younger, you used to take me and my
    > sister to ballet practice. You used to pick us up in
    > that black pickup truck, we'd sit in the back seat
    > and watch you make funny faces in the mirror.
    > When you dropped us off, you gave us a slobbery
    > kiss goodbye.

2. We sat there rotting, worms beneath our skin.
    > I don't remember when it ended. But I remember
    > the afters. The birthdays left unwished, the
    > Christmases with a single plastic card that soon
    > became only empty hands. Each holiday passing
    > by and not a word from you we heard.

———————•—————◦◦◦·◦◦◦————•———————

Robin Williams

3. You are all but decomposed.

> June twentieth twenty-twenty-one you invited us to a cookout. We talked about my future and where you'd like to live out the rest of yours. Sat in the shade of the trees I haven't seen since I was a girl and pretended there wasn't a lifetime missing between us.

4. You lead me onto the shore. We stared out at the water.

> Dad wished you a happy birthday, a wish that was long overdue. Everyone is grasping at straws, trying to make amends, right their wrongs. The hot air these days feels suffocating and time refuses to slow down for us.

WHAT I WOULD SAY IF THERE WERE NO CONSEQUENCES:

I'd say I hate you./ But not you, exactly./ I'd say I hate you for
hiding / for going three years and keeping me a secret / for
pretending like you were alone and had no one to call.//
I'd say I regret you./ But not you, exactly./ I'd say I regret you for
not being honest / for stringing me on for three months to knot
me up in a misunderstanding / for having me go 800 miles to
have you be late for the first hour.//
I'd say fuck you./ But not you exactly./ I'd say fuck you for the
hurt you put me through / for that night you made me cry on
the bathroom floor at one in the morning / for making me
believe that we were forever.//
I'd say I'm sorry./ But not for me, exactly./ I'd say I'm sorry for
putting all the blame on you / for the number of arguments that
could've ended if I wasn't so petty / for making you believe that
we were forever.//

————————

Robin Williams

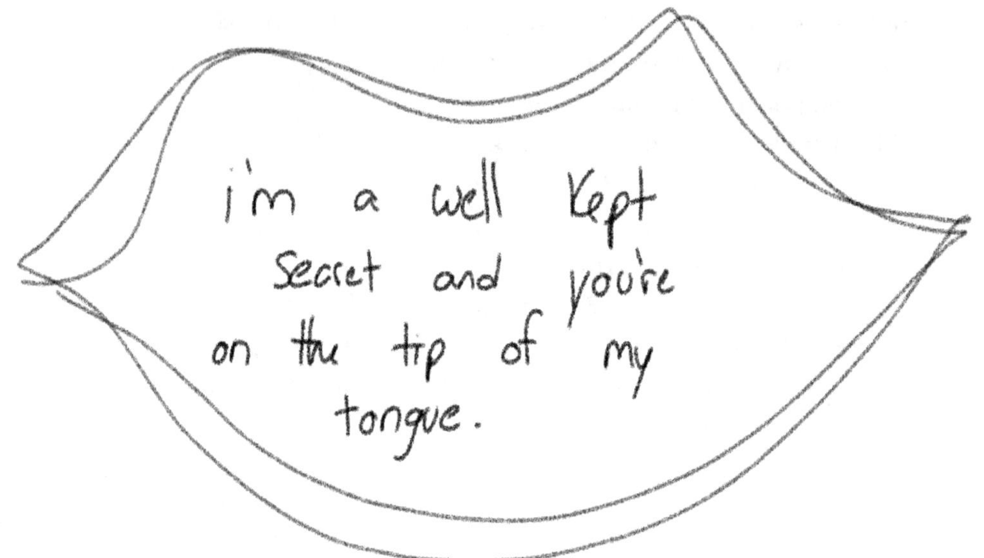
i'm a well kept
secret and you're
on the tip of my
tongue.

the lines between denying and bargaining are blurred together
everything is blurred together
kind of like how it is without your glasses on
blurry, unrecognizable, different

the more i look back, the hazier things get.
i knew it was over.
i was the one that said it was,
on impulse sure,
and i did try to take it back

and i don't really remember what i said.
all i remember is crying
and you talking
calmly
almost perfectly
as if nothing bothered you

(and maybe nothing did bother you;
you were waiting for this opportunity to strike again.)

i don't remember what hurt more:
me leaving you
or
you leaving me (five months before.)

———— ⋙∙⋘ ————

Robin Williams

I wanted a boy to kiss my scars
Not give me new ones

I romanticized that anyways too

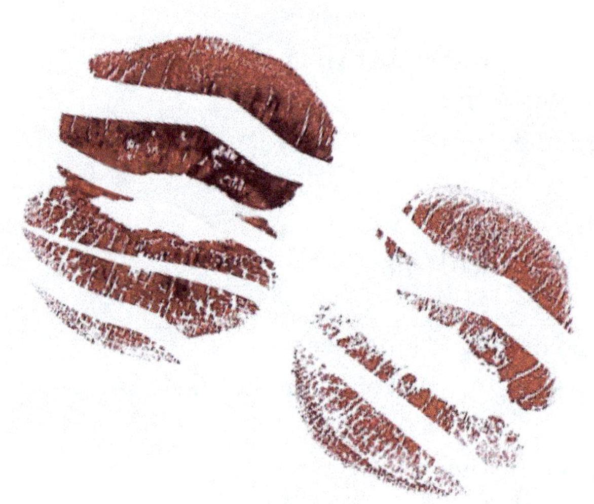

———◦◦◦·◦◦◦———
Robin Williams

The Edge ———————— of Hope

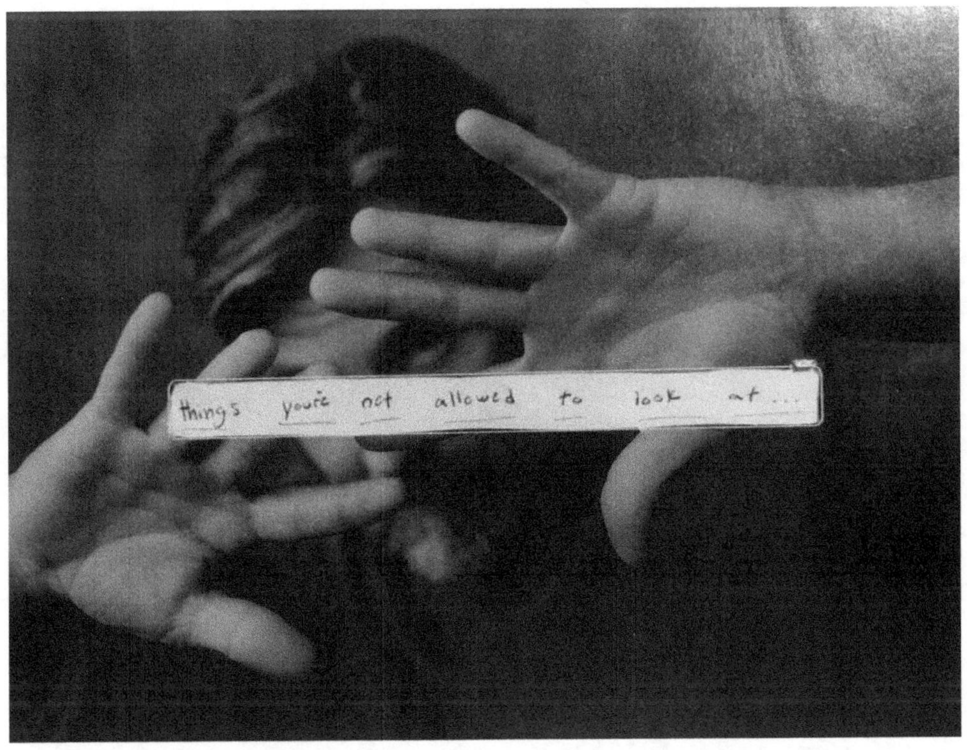

Robin Williams

THINGS YOU ARE NOT ALLOWED TO LOOK AT
after Skyler Saunders

The spider making its web in the ceiling corner of your room. The boy at the lunchroom table that you had a crush on. The eyes of your pastor as she tells you you're going to hell. Your best friend after you tell her you love her. Your tbr shelf as your mouse hovers over your cart. Pictures of you with long hair, or the mirror of yourself with short, because nothing will ever grow with the longing to cut it off.

Robin Williams

THINGS I WILL FORGET

The message I opened but never replied to.
To read my mother's note before work.
The sound of her voice. Her smile.
Her conversations about the shoe store and
the boys she was so over. To put the cap on
my ink bottle before it spills over. His
address. His favorite songs. The way they
liked their coffee. Where I put my glasses.
Where I left my keys. If I turned the shed
light off or not and if I even had the
power on. What my brother did to me.
The pain. The fear. These feelings of
worthlessness.

Robin Williams

Have you ever drowned under murky water?
Where your hands held onto plants
that slipped like slime through your fingers
as you tried to break the algae covered surface
for air?

No?
Me neither.

But it feels like I did,
that day I left school for the hospital
and couldn't see anything past the pouring of my tears.

A million eyes looked at me in that room
like a million eyes do when you're under unknown waters,
watching and waiting,
observing your next move.

I hope those swamp creatures are proud of me
for digging myself out of the mud.
It was much easier to die there,

to lie there,
than it was to tell the truth in the courtroom.

──────⚬⚬·⚬⚬──────

Robin Williams

the need to survive lit a fire in me
        after Rupi Kaur

they asked me to put it out. no, they begged me to.
got on their hands and knees and prayed I would,
just so they could have their happy little family back.

but there was no happy little family.

I was suffering for years, trying to claw my way out of a hole of water,
mud falling back down each time my fingernails scraped the top,
and now when I was finally able to take a breath—to take a stand—
I was "just trying to get back at him."

—maybe the truth would extinguish these flames.

————⊷∞∊·∍∞⊷————

Robin Williams

I tell people I'm healing,
that I've healed,
and there's nothing to worry about;
As I jot down every healing crystal known to man
say it's for the pretty colours
before putting it in my mouth
d
o
w
n
my t h r o a t
and in the   of my stomach
            pit

Can I heal myself from the inside out?

Robin Williams

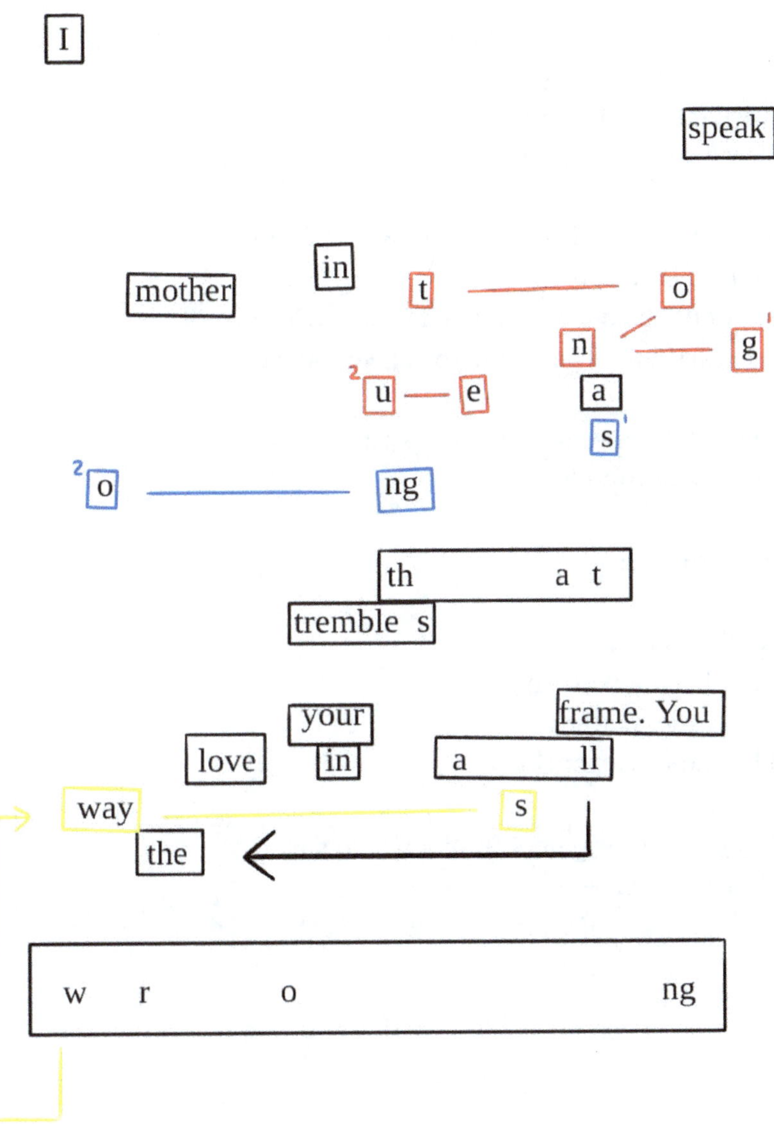
I
speak
in
mother
t
o
n
g
u e
a
s
2 o
ng
th   a t
tremble s
your
frame. You
love
in
a   ll
way
s
the
w   r   o   ng

<u>That's not loving someone.</u>
<u>I know.</u>

Jo March is so sick of being lonely
and I sometimes wonder
if I was in love with him.
Or was it just the idea of him?

I published my first book when I was sixteen,
fell in love then too.
I threw out the pages and tried to make love work,
three years later, everything has been burned.

I tried to fill the void with faceless love,
went against myself.
"So hot, so sexy,
send more nudes."

My body was praised,
my heart remained empty.
But they kept coming back,
and I loved the attention.

<u>If they asked me again, I think I would say</u>
No. I hated it all.

——————⋗⊃◯⊂·⊃◯⊂⋖——————

Robin Williams

A Series of Drafts I Will Never Finish pt. 1

> ➤ My worries wrapped around my shoulders like a neck pillow on a plane trip to Florida. Nowhere to run, thousands of feet up into the air, all the room to let them tumble down, past the clouds below me. But I hold onto them anyway, my head against the window.

> ➤ I sink my head under the water to drown out the noise
> But it doesn't work
> Of course, it doesn't work
> I can't escape what's inside my head

> ➤ First name friend last name nothing to worry about
> First name never last name will you break my heart again

> ➤ I am nothing more than broken universe and that doesn't make me special

> ➤ Shouldn't God be the one asking for forgiveness

————⊷⊶·⊷⊶————

Robin Williams

"I date women. It can be a choice."

Dear woman, being gay is not a choice.

I didn't choose to have panic attacks when my brother told the whole girls lacrosse team I was gay. I didn't choose to break down in tears when my grandmother told me it didn't matter, she still loved me. I didn't choose to be baptized into a church that had an entire filing system dedicated to teaching me I was the worst of sinners.

I did choose that man with the long, blond hair. I did choose the girl with soft brown eyes. I did choose to turn down the man with the scuffed sneakers playing soccer, and that girl with the crescent moon tattoo on the back of her neck.

They are not the same, and saying they are, is a harmful thing.

So, dear woman with 30k followers,
Please be mindful of your words.

Robin Williams

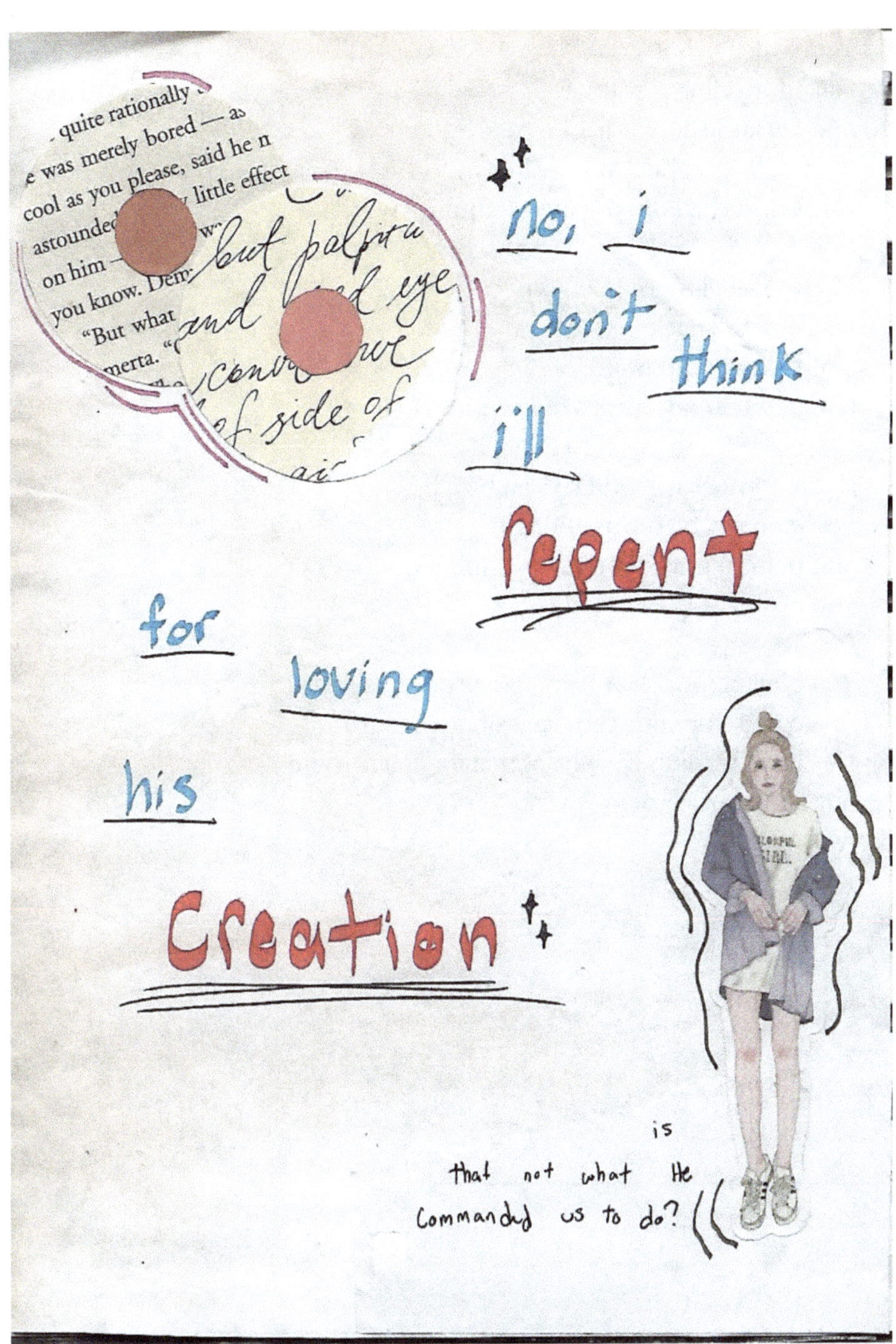
no, i
don't think
i'll
repent
for
loving
his
creation
is
that not what He
commanded us to do?

Your voice echoes,
locked inside the mirror,
and I stand there staring
at the silver reflecting my body,
reflecting the pain of your wounding words.

I leave the camera flash on,
wait for the click
and I exhale the breath
trapped behind my gritted teeth.

Come tomorrow I will twirl a brush
between my bitten-nail fingers
and paint a portrait of everything I am
and everything I am not.

You played me like a game of cards
made only for your time-passing pleasure
and I will remain the ace of hearts
but I will not remain yours.

Robin Williams

We were pieces of
a different puzzle
trying
to   fit
into each other's c
                    u
            r
        v
es
Each missing the
        center,
a hole in
        wh at sho uld be comp lete

————⋈∙⋈————
Robin Williams

the day i stopped giving a fuck was the day i stopped being your babe

and *god* it's been wonderful

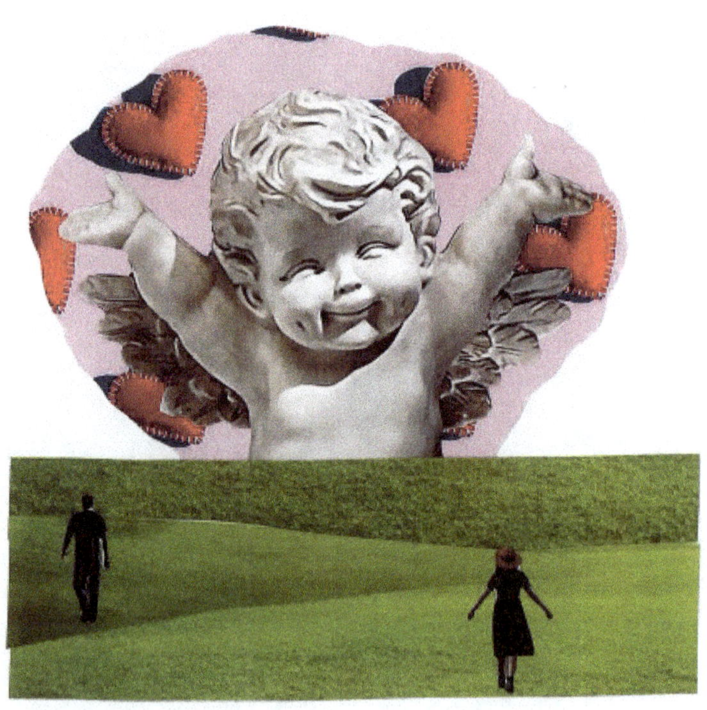

See,

There was no reason to call it love,
it was far from it.

I would have died for you because I loved you,
you would've died because you hated the thought of me leaving.

I shouldn't have cared,
should have left you on read,
should have blocked your number,
turned away and never came back

but me and my stupid little heart
needed someone to love me—

Even if there was no reason to call it love,
because it wasn't.

It was only hurting.

————⟩∞⟨·⟩∞⟨————

Robin Williams

for a long time i was angry with you
for a long time i was hurt
and maybe i still am,
just a little angry, hurt.
everytime i think about the things you said to me
everytime i think about how you said you loved me

everytime i think about you

it feels like i'm drowning in a fit of rage
that maybe you don't deserve.
but maybe you do.

which one of us was the monster
in this love turned nightmare?

———————•OC · OO•———————

Robin Williams

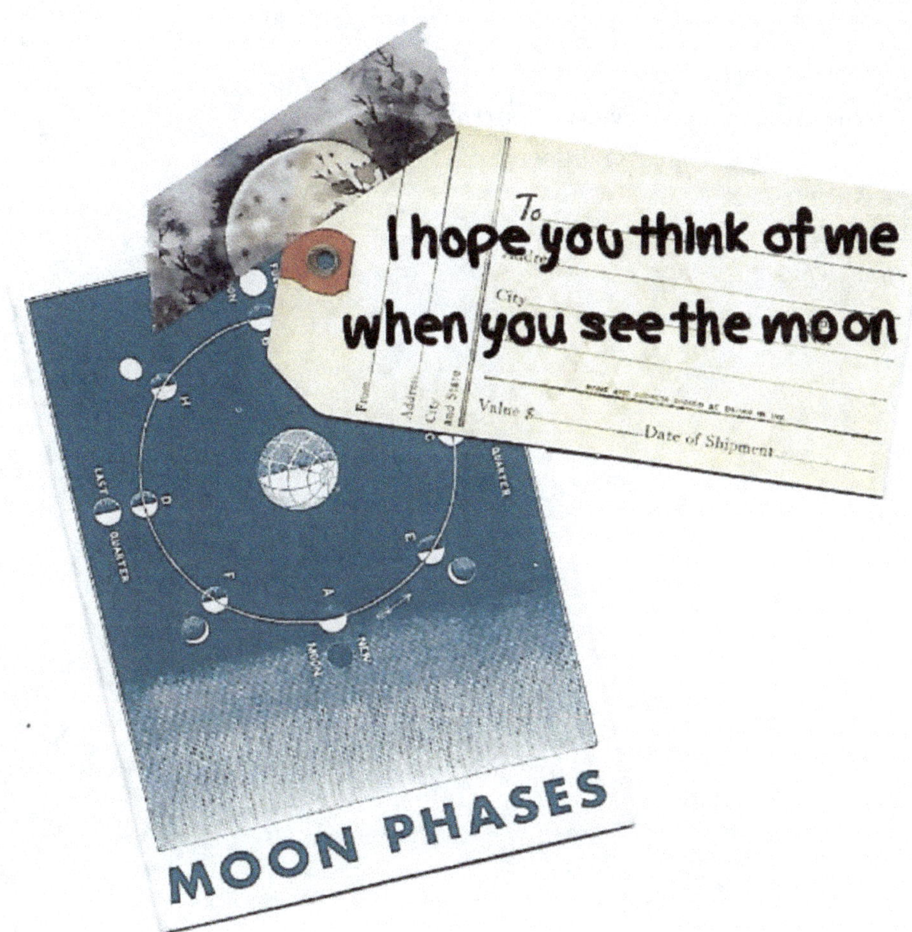
MOON PHASES
To
I hope you think of me
when you see the moon
Date of Shipment
Value $

What sweet revenge,

the moon we slept under,
fell in love with together,
stared at in awe on that very first night,

will forever haunt you,
peering through your window curtains
as you wonder what you did wrong.

Go ask her.
Go ask her.

Robin Williams

the ways you cheated on me told through the colours of a bruise

red: You said I was insecure, overreacting, untrusting. You said it hurt you, the way I thought you weren't loyal, broke you inside. You said you loved me and would never go behind my back, that I had nothing to worry about. We broke up and two days later you're letting her suck your dick, letting her kiss your lips. You let her be your everything when it was supposed to be me. You said you wouldn't cheat, but you're a liar. You're a fucking liar.

purple: I sometimes wonder how I came up in the conversation. Did you accidentally say my name when you were whispering into her ear? I sometimes wonder how she reacted. Was she mad? Hurt? Confused? I want you to know she wasted no time between your stuttering to tell me, admission left her lips in the blink of an eye. I sometimes wonder if she was afraid I'd be upset with her for actions that were all your fault. I hope she knows I'm thankful for her. She helped me realize what a shit person you were.

yellow: I bet her lip gloss tasted like strawberries, sweet and soft and red. I bet you enjoyed every moment, with her arms wrapped around your neck, with your hands on her waist. I bet you felt the world give out beneath your feet, your heart drop to the pit of your stomach. Does the moment I caught you still haunt you? I hope it does. I hope every girl you kiss tastes like strawberries and reminds you of me.

brown: I look back on all the second chances I gave my lovers before, and part of me feels sorry I never let you get yours. But when it became blatantly obvious you were going behind my back, beyond his name being in your bio with a lock and key, like a middle schooler's first relationship, I had to treat myself right. Because you wouldn't, you didn't, and I've learned that the hard way, time and time before.

I'm clinging on to a memory
Afraid to let you go
Or maybe I'm just afraid to love anyone else
Because it hurt to love you
But it hurt even more to lose you
And I don't want to put myself through that again

Robin Williams

How many forevers are in a lifetime?
Because I'm convinced I wasted all of mine on you.

The first one fell down the drain with my tears
and hair and all the soap I used
to try and pretty myself up for you.
It mixed itself with toothpaste and "I'm sorrys"
for never being good enough.
You said she was just a friend.

The second one was taken by the waitress at Hoss's.
She gave me a clean, clear ~~conscience~~ plate
and told me to fill myself up with sweets.
Maybe the sugar would numb the pain behind a chemical bliss.
You never told me about her.

The third forever slipped between our fingers.
But you can't convince me we didn't just drop it.
You left it at your feet months before I let it go.
You said I convinced you, then, to stay.
But I couldn't now.

And damn I tried.
Every night
for a straight week.

But our forevers
became never(s) again

———— ⋈⋄⋈ ————

Robin Williams

{ <title>
</ERROR>

<by=[robin williams]>

<question> </beginning>
*what happened?

<form> </answer> </middle>
<input>
*we fell in love when we were sixteen <incorrect input>
*the distance was the problem <incorrect input>
*young love just doesn't last <incorrect input>
*she was a friend she was a friend she was a friend <incorrect input>
*it was simply the right person wrong time <incorrect input>
*we were both busy with work, with school, with our lives <incorrect input>

<error>
*you have reached the maximum number of ~~<excuses>~~ invalid inputs.
*please try again later.

<form> </answer> </end>
<input>
*he didn't love me.

<input correct> }

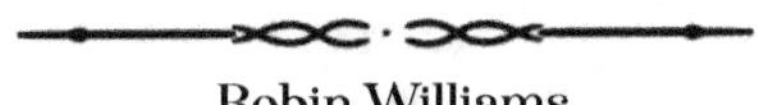

Robin Williams

i'm   left   with

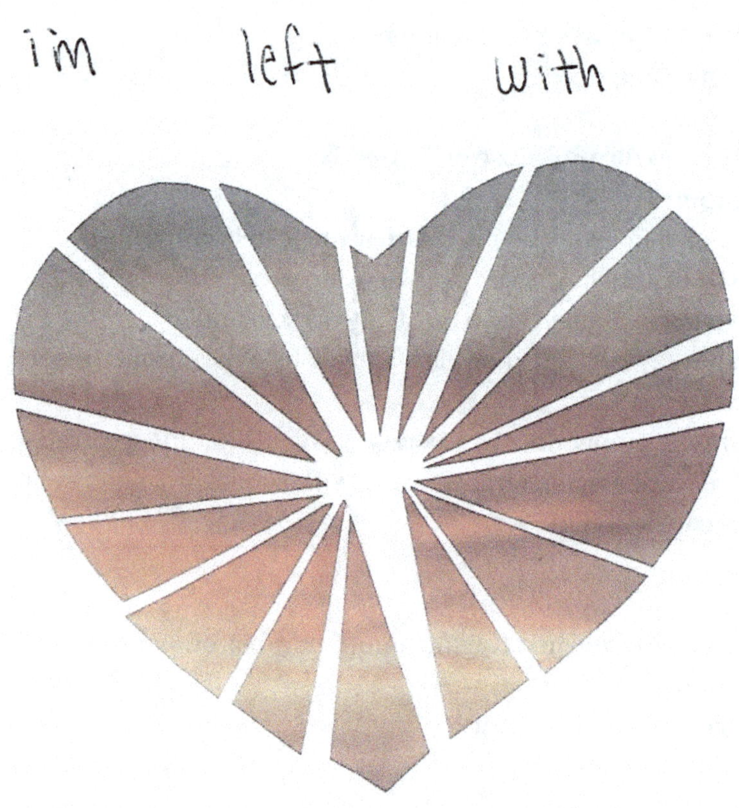

a   Kaleidoscope

heart

Let this be a poem and not an apology...

Let this be a phone call during a thunderstorm and not a
confession.
Let this be a song on the radio and not a plea out of my mouth.
Let this be a moment of healing, of flowers blooming on a warm
summer day and not my parents thanking me for forgiving you.
Let this be a poem for me and not an apology to you.

Robin Williams

it's been a little over a year since your verdict was decided
and i still don't know
how to feel

i believe i am less angry now than i was then,

but the boil inside of me
when i hear you're not liking your probation officer,
or that you got a good paying job,
begs to differ with my beliefs.

or perhaps it's just jealousy and less rage
that i feel expected
to care about your comfort in a punishment
i fight with myself over being too light or not.

that i feel expected
to be happy for your life that has begun to move forward
after months of hearing frustration pouring from lips at the
dinner table

about how you
almost
had that job

about how you
almost
had a friend

———————•≻○⊂·⊃○≺•———————

Robin Williams

about how you
almost
began to move your life forward on your own

when i chose my career at sixteen and stuck to it,
applied for jobs, queried to agents, submitted to presses,
and it was not even close to an
almost
of anything

Robin Williams

an·ger
/ˈaNGgər/

noun

1. A strong feeling of annoyance, displeasure, or hostility.
2. A strong feeling that never leaves, just stays dormant in my bones.
3. Red cheeks, burning cheeks. Crying, lots of crying. Sometimes yelling, sometimes silence.
4. A strong feeling I feel when I think of him. Play Guess Who: Who is him?
5. Late nights with my sister, talking in anything but whispers, about him. I never get to finish my sentence. It's a run on,
6. It will always be a run on,
7. I will always be angry with him.

Looking back at certain pieces
I realize I tend to have a lot to say
for someone who'd rather not speak much at all
about a certain court case
and certain emotions
from that certain court case
towards a certain someone

and there's always a single thought bouncing around in my head,

When will I be done writing this story?

———∞·∞———

Robin Williams

Date

M

Address

Reg. No.	Clerk	Account Forward	
1	How long do		
2			
3	i have to		
4			
5	wait till i		
6			
7	forget all		
8			
9	of our		
10			
11			
12			
13			
14			
15			

memories

A-1200/85
T-45202/

...unt Stated to Date - If Error Is Found, Return at Once

I met a boy in June. His favorite colour is green and he'd eat apples as the only fruit for the rest of his life. He played Clair de Lune for me countless times, each rendition more perfect than the last.

Three months in, he broke my heart. I felt lost, betrayed, and used. I said things I now regret. I forgave and tried to forget.

Three years later, I broke his heart. I admitted I never forgot, and I struggled to forgive. I felt afraid, I felt guilty, and convinced him I'd change, and I did just that. He forgave and tried to forget.

Three months later, we broke our hearts. He was hurt, I was angry, we were the downfall of ourselves and each other. I wish we could forgive and forget.

I said goodbye to a boy in June. I'm trying to forget his favorite characters in the movies he loved and burn the memories from my mind. I'm trying to see a future without him, but each day hurts more than the last.

Robin Williams

I don't hold fond memories of us

Walking laps at football games
pretending we knew what was going on.
Spilling buckets of popcorn
under movie theater seats.
Blueberries and chocolate chip pancakes
on a bench at the lake.
The bronze flower necklace chain
you insisted on struggling to put around my neck.

Stopping you from punching
the bright brick walls each time our team lost,
splitting the skin on your knuckles.
Arguing about respecting my boundaries
in hushed voices, getting angry side glances
from the people in front of us.
The empty parking lot,
your car gone, me, alone,
watching the geese pick through the breakfast scraps.

Your refusal to
let me
let you
go

Robin Williams

My chest dropped into the pit of my stomach; you didn't want to be together. Words of desperation fell off my lips.

I loved you and I was convinced I would never love anyone else. I loved you and I am convinced I will never love anyone else. It's been a year and I can't love anyone else.

But you have moved on and life will continue to move on and move on and move on and move on and move on and move on and move on and move on and move on and move on and move on and move on and move on and move on and move on and move on and move on and move on and move on and move on on on on on on on on on on on on on on on on on on on

on

on

on

on

My body feels like a scorched landscape clawing at the soil for a drop of water. What have I done, leaving you?

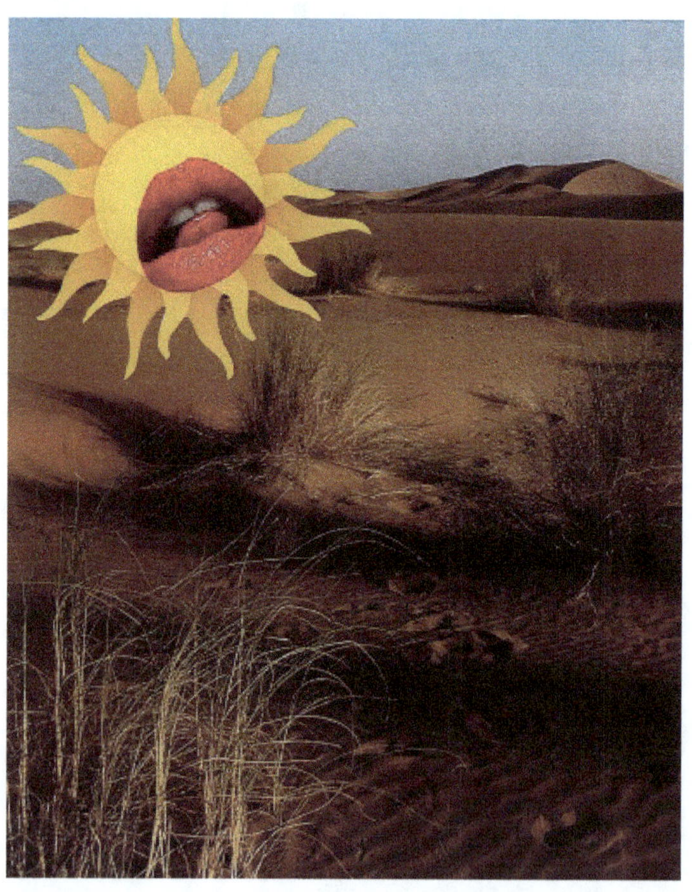

Robin Williams

i want nothing more than to wrap my arms around you

i want to rip the hands off the clock, make time go back, have the
sun rise and not set, just this once
just this
once

i want to dream the impossible, to achieve it, to live it all once
more
even if only for a few seconds
i want nothing
tick
more than to
tick
wrap my arms
tick
around you
ding

Robin Williams

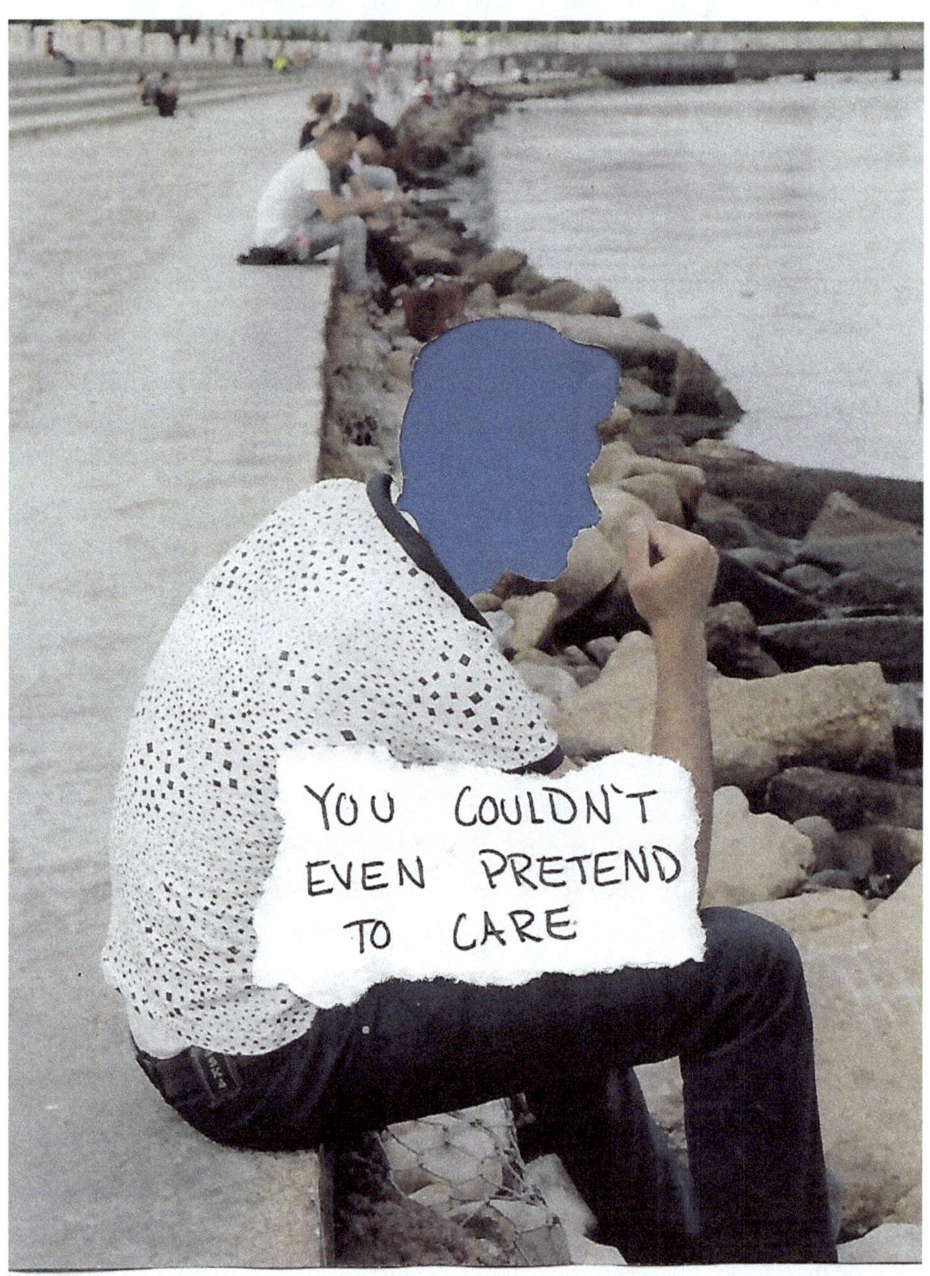
YOU COULDN`T
EVEN PRETEND
TO CARE

I spent nights crying,
never sleeping,
working with circles under my eyes
and tissues in my pockets,
hiding in the bathroom every ten minutes
to silence my pain

while you stood there,
perfectly unfazed.

Even now, I'm the only one who cares.

11/09/15

I called you up to talk,
I missed hearing your voice
and I thought you missed me, too.
But you picked up with silence on the line
and didn't answer me when I said hello.

Moments went by before
I confessed why I really called.
I wanted to know why you weren't trying,
why you gave up on us,
why you told all our friends that I was ignoring you, ghosting you.

I wanted to know what I did to deserve the least of your best,
when I'd given all of me to keep you happy,
gave yesses when I wanted to give nos.

You said five words,
hung up the phone,
and left me crying on my bathroom floor.

——————⊸✕⊂ · ⊃✕⊷——————

Robin Williams

I press beautiful flowers under immense weight
so I can hold their beauty forever in scrapbook pages.

Perhaps that is what I've done to her,

put on pressure to stay this way forever,
to look good in pond reflections.

Perhaps that is what broke her,

the pressure to be afraid of change
when it was what I needed to grow,

to blossom.

    —to my younger self, i'm sorry

I only came back to you
because I was scared
of change

Robin Williams

what is left of me if i have no more pain,
no more hurt to stamp onto the pages,
no more words to share about them?

————⟡⟡————
Robin Williams

It creeps up on me in the early late hours when I least expect it,
when I'm lying in bed, on a car ride home, in a mall surrounded
by strangers.

Out of nowhere it pounces, carves my heart out in a clean swipe,
and tears it apart ever so slowly.

It forces me to watch, helpless, while I cry and cry and cry.

This hurting from a love I can no longer hold
it just doesn't want to leave.

——————⊰⊙⊂·⊃⊙⊱——————
Robin Williams

I measure my worth in the numbers of words, the number of
pages, the number of books held together by glue and staples
and paperclips.

Just as I measure my worth in the number of times she says she
loves me, the number of ways she kisses me, the number of
messages she sends when on the road, when at work, when
beside me.

I asked for a love to write about, asked for a new muse and I
found her, and I loved her, and I lost her, and I want to move past
her.

But when I do, what will be left of me?
What am I worth when I have numbers of nothing?

———⚬•⚬———

Robin Williams

**i opened a fortune cookie one afternoon and it said something to
the effect of, "do what you love to do,"**
after Parker Lee

i opened a fortune cookie one afternoon and it said something to
the effect of, "do what you love to do,"

so i opened a blank document and waited.
i opened the window and let the soft winds and wisps blow in.
i listened to the birds chirp and hop around on fallen leaves.

i sat there,
a warm cup of chai in my hands,
and i wrote.

Robin Williams

A TIMELINE OF A THIEFS LIFE:

Birth: When people ask me what my lucky number is, I tell them 22. I was born in October, on the twenty-second. Ten. Twenty. Two. Three "T"s on the day you were born seems kind of lucky, no? Born less than a pound, fitting in the palm of my father's hand, my mother pushing months too early: they said I was a miracle. I don't feel like one. I feel like a thief of life. Taking what isn't mine. Some baby somewhere else could've needed my air. I stole their breath.

Life: Small. Shy. Ask me what my favorite colour is: black. Introverted. Anxious. Ask me what my favorite pastime is: reading. I have amounted to nothing but a closet of secrets. My wardrobe hid me and a collection of tomboyish attire, and sometimes a razor. But I don't like to think about the cold dark nights. My parents are expecting something that I cannot give them: a son-in-law. I don't feel like that. I feel like a thief of love. Taking what isn't mine. Some family somewhere else could've needed this love. I stole their child.

Death: Sitting around the living room, politics on TV, someone says something. I say something to someone. Went a little like: "You're going to have to start caring because I am one of them." One of who? "Them. I'm bisexual." You're what? "I like guys. And I like girls." I can't tell you which parent sighed the hardest or who said what after, seems they've come around though.

———⋈done·done⟨———

Robin Williams

I called my grandmother up. She answered the phone, told her I had something to say. She waited. Went a little like: "I'm bisexual. I like guys and I like girls." Okay? What do you want me to say? "I don't know. I wanted to tell you." I still love you. You're my granddaughter, I will always love you. "You do?" I can't tell you what happened after, other than I cried. They all said it was okay. I don't feel okay. I feel different, lighter. Some angel somewhere else could've needed this light. I stole their wings.

Rebirth: When people ask me what my lucky number is, I tell them 22. But not because that was the day I was born, no. But because that was the day I lived, honestly, the first and thought-to-be last time. Open and vulnerable to a world I didn't know. I have spent the past of my life living as somebody else, a thief, thinking I stole what wasn't mine to have. It's now, ten twenty-two in the morning, and I just told the world I was bisexual.

all the things i wish i
said
knew how to say
had the chance to say

but couldn't

i think i've found
the words
the time
to say it all
now

Robin Williams

A Series of Drafts I Will Never Finish pt. 2
I Made Loving You My Religion

➢ I made loving you my religion

Maybe it was because I was told finding love was like
finding heaven
like finding a home after running for so long
like finding a metal overhang to hide under from the
pouring rain
like finding the words to that song you've been humming
all day

All day, humming that song from Sunday worship
The congregation praising a man
for putting the stars in the sky
and breath into their lungs

You took my breath away
Every moment I heard your voice
➢ My grandmother could swear you were the devil and
with the way my cheeks burned she might not be wrong
➢ I was on fire and
I was in love with you
➢ I didn't see you as some perfect God who could do no
wrong, no
I knew better than to expect that from anyone

But I do see you as the creator of my world
Of my new life that you forged barehanded out of empty
darkness and a small orb of light

————⋙⊂·⊃⋘————
Robin Williams

Texts I Will Never Send pt. 2

1. I still think of the way you smile. It still makes me smile.
2. Sending you that Christmas card, hearing that you loved it, made me the happiest I've been in awhile.
3. It's good to hear your voice, to see your face.
4. It feels like I've got my best friend back. It feels like we're okay again.
5. Thank you for the happiest years of my life.

Robin Williams

31 mins (19 miles)

Best route now due to ~~heartbreak~~ traffic conditions

- Your location:

You're sitting on your living room floor, picking cat whiskers out of seat cushions, making wishes, and tossing them onto the carpet to find another day. You're waiting for the holidays to end so your emptiness can end.

- Head northeast onto Christmas Card Purchases toward Empty Envelopes Addressed to Him

You've stopped crying in August and there was comfort in the world outside dying while you laid hollow in your bed. You scroll through your social media feed, tapping on ads and closing out. There will be no gifts this year and your wallet oddly misses the taste of paying for his things.

- Turn left onto God Not This Again

You've stopped crying in August, or so you thought. Everyone is giddy and all smiles, singing carols in the backseat, but you can't be happy without your heart in your chest. You're crying again. Your friend tells you healing isn't linear. You tell them to fuck off. You don't apologize.

- ~~Swipe~~ Turn right onto Matches But No Match

Despite feeling sick every time you think of kissing him, you feel grateful to be alone. You've known your identity, and now it has been cemented in every man swiped left, but you can't bring yourself to date her. You ask for his permission. He says he doesn't care; we're not dating anymore. You don't need permission.

——————◦◦◦◦————————

Robin Williams

- In the next two months turn slightly right onto I'm
  Feeling Okay Again/But I Know I Won't Tomorrow

You've gone on a few dates, cut off all your hair, went to court, and still found yourself breathing when you declared you wouldn't ever again. But the calendar says March, and you want to forget, yet you wish him a happy birthday anyways.

- In the next two days turn left onto Exes Can Still Be
  Friends

You're not mad at him anymore. In fact, you've sobered up to realize there was nobody to blame for the fallout. You've apologized and moved

on and spend your conversations being called out for simping over Padme. You laugh together and everything feels good, everything feels normal, everything feels like it did before you fell in love.

- Your destination will be on the right:

It's been a year since your anniversary stopped being an anniversary and instead just another day on the fridge calendar. You've made a list of friends to gift presents to this Christmas. You're sitting on your living room floor, picking cat whiskers out of the seat cushions, making wishes, and tossing them onto the carpet to be found again. You're waiting for the holidays to start so you can send him his card.

Robin Williams

There's nothing I want more than

To stare up at the stars on a windy night in the first week of December, watching them twinkle like the lights on the house next door.

To take pictures of hair past my shoulders, pulled back behind my ears by a red bow, with a cliche caption "*merry christmas, i got you a gift: me.*"

To sing Coldplay songs at the top of our lungs with the windows down, your hand on my shoulder as you take a dramatic lead, singing the words I only know how to mumble.

To run my fingers through your hair, watching old vines on your phone, holding that feeling of love in the palms of my hand.

There's nothing I want more than
                          You

———•———⋈⚭·⚭⋊———•———

Robin Williams

Time doesn't slow down

It doesn't give you the chance to catch your breath,
doesn't give you a moment longer to say goodbye.
It doesn't wait for you to be ready to take on the next day.

You cannot stand on the edge of hope,
praying for it to see your way,
to give you the perfect minute to say what you need to say.

Time doesn't slow down.

Say it—
Do it—
Go after it—

Tell them you love them.
Tell them you appreciate them.
Hug them and don't let go,

before it's the last time
you ever get the chance to.

———— ⚬⚬⚬·⚬⚬⚬ ————
Robin Williams

I remember how you told me to stand in front of a mirror and
tell myself that I was beautiful and worthy ten times each
morning.
I did it once, felt uncomfortable looking at the odd shapes on my
face, and never did it again.
But I lied and told you I did, thanked you for growing my
confidence.
Now, almost four years later, I have the biggest ego.
I know that I am beautiful, and I know that I am worthy.

I don't apologize for taking up space.

After we broke up,
I had no idea who I was.
In one moment,
I was surrounded by light, and in the next,
a sharp gust snuffed out each candle
and I was left in the dark, lost.

It took me months to just begin to
understand what I liked without your influence,
what brought me joy on my own.
I stopped marking the days
on a piece of found driftwood
and just let myself exist.

I still haven't quite figured out who I am,
but I have a better grasp now.

I can look in a mirror without seeing
the ghost of you over my shoulder,
I am more pieced together than hollow,
and that dusty rose colour
has returned to my cheeks
in that monochrome photo.

Robin Williams

It was in the morning after,
when the frost hadn't left the grass
and the air was crisp in my lungs,
that I reminded myself it wasn't a question of
why wasn't I enough?
but a question of
why couldn't she be better
at treating me—
loving me—
right?

Robin Williams

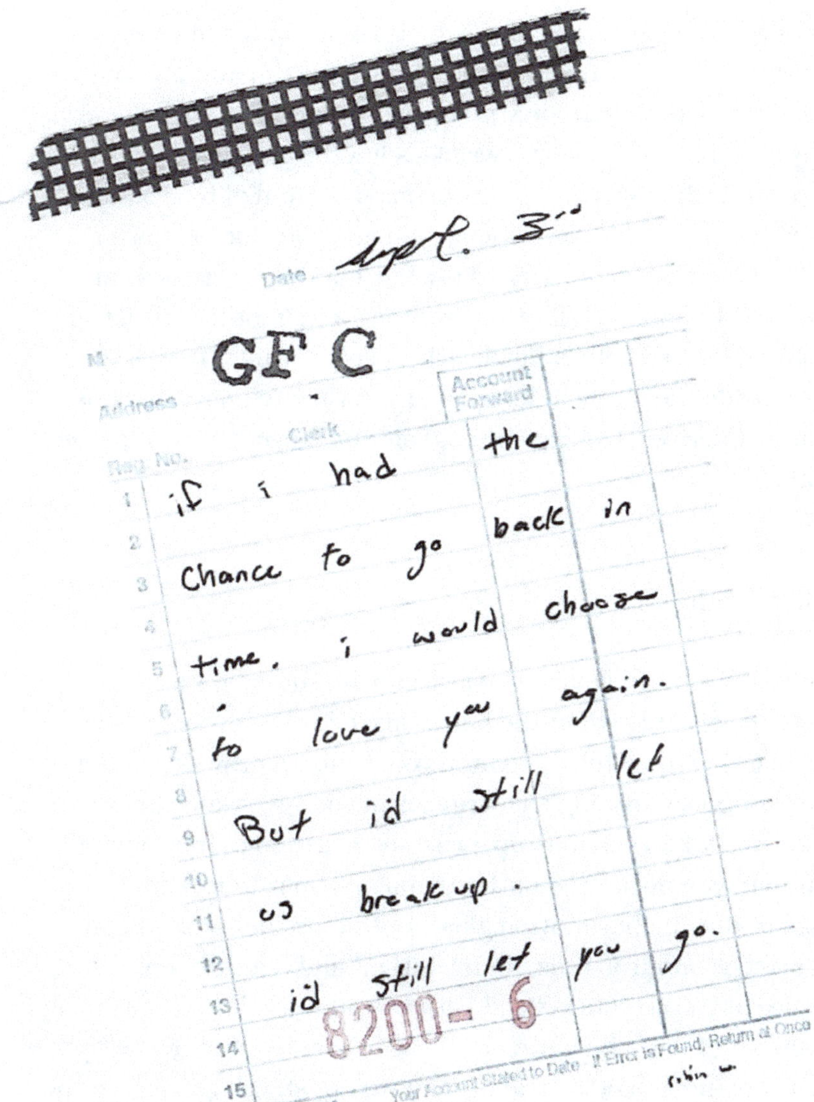

Robin Williams

Earth

The sky has been cloudy all week, sunlight dipping its toes onto the sidewalk only when she has to leave for the evening. She doesn't stay to watch me watch you. Under a grey sky, under a grey lamppost, ironing the wrinkles in your grey knee length skirt. And when you look up, brushing a strand of hair behind your ear, you notice me noticing you and your foot steps out from under the bus station glass. But before our strides can connect, a raindrop falls, then another, and another, until the silence of the streets is filled with the pit pat pit. I turn to go back inside the dimly lit lobby, and you turn to board the bus that just arrived, locking the cold air out. Never to cross paths again.

Other Earth

The sky has been cloudy all week, sunlight dipping its toes onto the sidewalk only when she has to leave for the evening. She doesn't stay to watch me watch you. Under a grey sky, under a grey lamppost, ironing the wrinkles in your grey knee length skirt. And when you look up, brushing a strand of hair behind your ear, you notice me noticing you and your foot steps out from under the bus station glass. But before our strides can connect, a raindrop falls, then another, and another, until the silence of the streets is filled with the pit pat pit. Our eyes meet again, and I don't hesitate, my right foot in front of my left, your hair hanging in single strands, and we are standing so close the rain doesn't feel cold anymore. Everything feels warm.

———————◦⋈⋊·⋉⋈◦———————

Robin Williams

do you remember the dr. pepper i spilled onto the seat of your car and how i never told you until months after?
do you remember the hand-drawn postcards i sent you, the hummingbird, and miscounted piano keys?
do you remember the time turner necklace you sent me on my 18th birthday, my most prized possession, even with the gold paint flaking off?
do you remember the time we planned to facetime while i ate a bagel to help get over my insecurities of eating in front of others?
do you remember how i told you i've never kissed anyone before and i was embarrassed to admit i wasn't even sure if i knew how to?
do you remember leaving the hotel while the sun went down, standing under the roof out-peak waiting for one of us to say goodbye?
do you remember how you kissed me then, without a second thought?

i do, i do.

Robin Williams

Everything's been discovered, invented, done time and time before,

But you made this love something completely new.

rulers make bad lovers

but there's something about the way
you can command my body
to move in time with yours

even without song
your heartbeat keeps
perfect time

——•————⊃◯⊂·⊃◯⊂————•——
Robin Williams

The Edge ———— of Hope

It is in this moment

Red iron in my mouth
Man beneath my boot

Whispering memories
Of your lips on my neck
Hot breath down my spine

That I am in love with you.

Robin Williams

Dear Creator/God/Universe/Mother Nature,

I'm not one to pray but I hope you'll still listen, still answer this
call:

Can you tell them I love them?
No.
I don't *love* them anymore.

Can you tell them, instead,
that I cherish them/that I've forgiven them/that I think fondly
of the moments we shared?

Can you tell them
that I'm not that broken girl I used to be/that I'm healing/that
I'm working on myself/that I'm sorry for hurting them out of
frustration of my own pain and confusion?

Can you tell them
that I wish them a bright future/that I hope they go after their
dreams/that I'm rooting for them, always?

——————⬦○⬥ · ⬥○⬦——————
Robin Williams

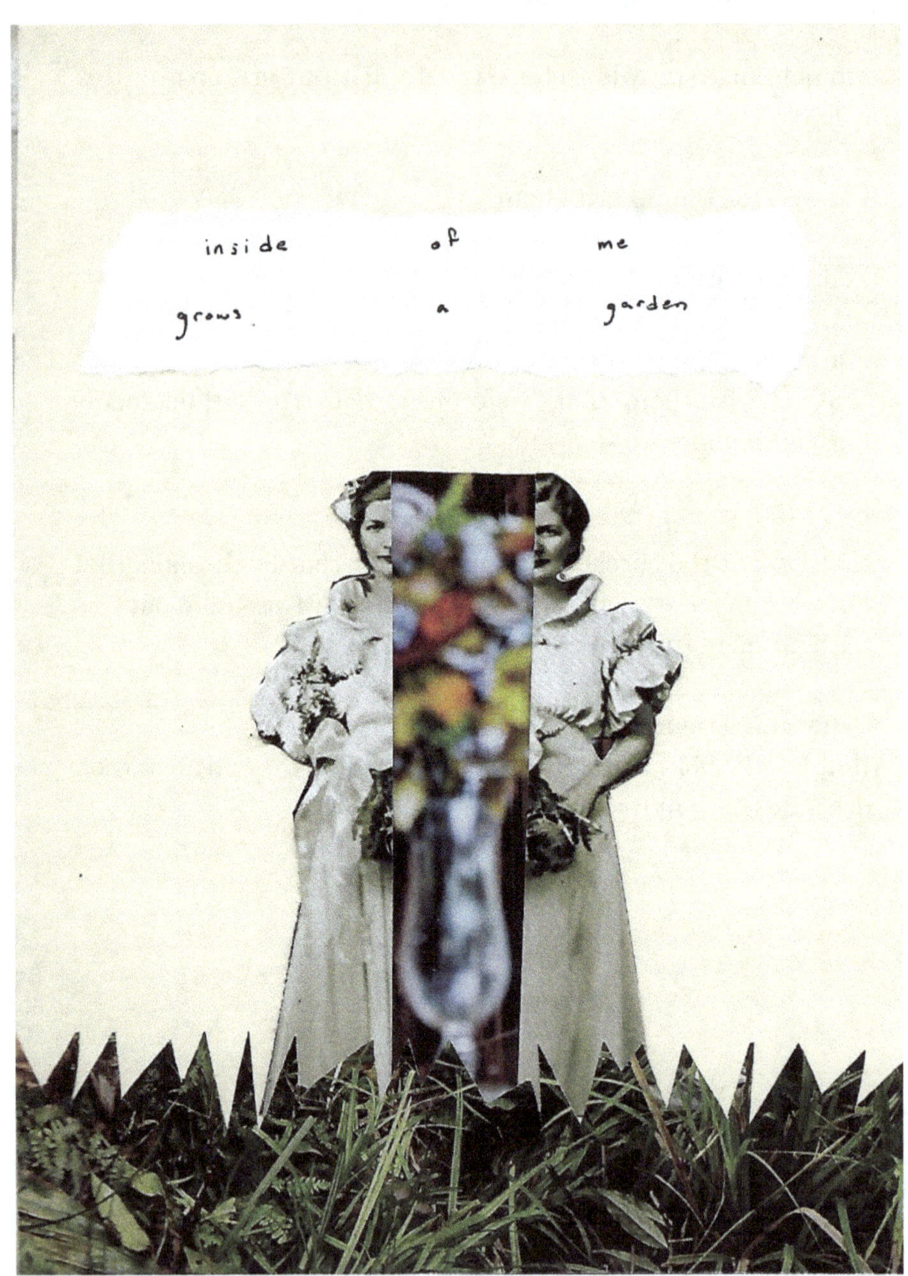
inside   of   me
grows   a   garden

Picking Petals Off Flowers/The Lessons I Learned

Sunflower: *a tall, yellow flower with seeds you roast, crack, spit, and eat, a sign of summertime*
It's hard to hold anger and sunflower petals in the same hand, to hold hurt in my heart while the bright petals dye my skin the happiest of colours. Instead, I crush the seeds under the heel of my boot, scoop them up in a tray, and drop them in the dustbin. One by one by one. Let's play a game of "~~they love me~~, they love me not."

(I don't want to make you out to be the bad guy again. *pluck* Out of all the rest, you were the better, you were the best. *crush* I can't get over some of the things you said, some of the things you did, it all still hurts. *toss* You're the only one I'd say yes to again. After all this time? Always. *repeat*)

Peony: *a fragrant flower, with many colour variations, that comes back every year*
I sit in the browning grass, a peony in my hand, another cluster at my feet. I crush the first petal between my thumb and forefinger, rolling it over, letting it bleed into the cracks of my fingernails. One by one by one. Let's play a game of "~~they love me~~, they love me not."

(*pick* Insanity is doing the same thing over again, knowing the outcome will never change, and choosing to do it anyways. *roll* A third chance won't make a difference if they stopped caring after the first. *bleed* A relationship takes two, not one, not just you. *repeat*)

──────•⟩∞⟨·⟩∞⟨•──────

Robin Williams

Rose: *a flower from prickly shrubs, most commonly grown in deep reds, found in bouquets given after arguments*

Thumb pricks are the same colour as the rose petals falling off the dying bouquet I keep on my bookshelf. I brought them home and stuffed them into an empty vase, hid them in the dark, and let them rot. Maybe I'll crush them into a blush for my cheeks when my career takes off, maybe I'll leave them at the grave of yours. For now, I continue to watch them fall. One by one by one. Let's play a game of "~~they love me~~, they love me not."

(You made love feel like torture. *watch* You always found somebody else to blame. *rot* Never knew how to apologize, just kept feeding me more lies. *fall* Told me I was nothing, would never be anything. Take a look at me now. *repeat*)

I never understood
how someone could love
someone for so long
and move on so fast
until I did.

And I realized that didn't mean
I never loved them
But that I did.

And because I loved them,
I had to move forward
for the sake of both of us.

Robin Williams

Getting Over You Means

forgetting your favorite songs/forgetting your favorite flower/not thinking of you when I hear someone play the piano/forgetting the way you tasted/forgetting how many times I've been cheated on/deleting the texts/the emails/the pictures/the notes/remembering the happy memories of high school football games/selling the ring and buying a better one for myself/watching my favorite things without you/without crying/without thinking of your voice in my ear/

Robin Williams

I don't know if you need to hear this
but I do:

Despite how much it hurt then,
and how much it hurts now,

you don't need to be afraid of walking through that door,
leaving it all behind you,
in the past where it should stay.

There is healing on the other side,
there is light and
there is hope and
there is new love.

Staying on this side,
pretending it's locked,
while the key rusts sitting in the palm of your hand

only leaves you hurting,
only leaves you longing,
only leaves you replaying the movie
of a relationship you no longer star in.

I don't know if you need to hear this
but I do:

You can walk away whenever you want.

———⟩○⟨⟩○⟨———

Robin Williams

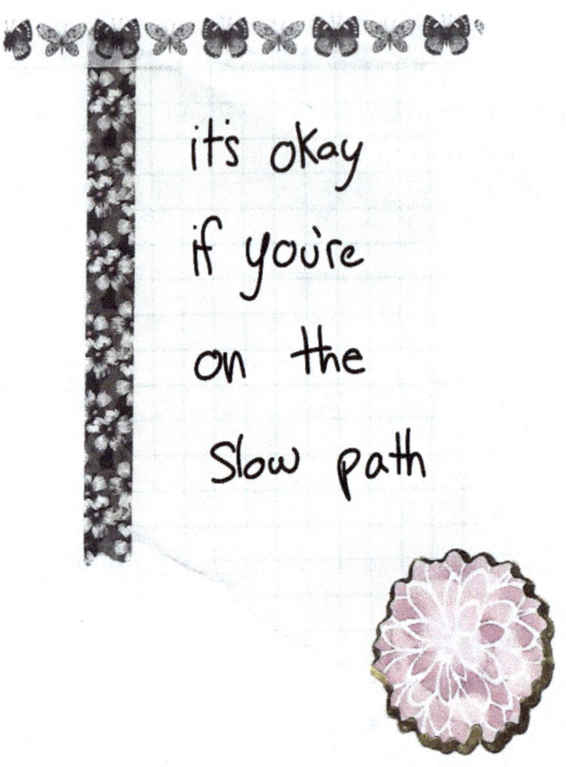
it's okay
if you're
on the
slow path

stay alive, that would be enough/small reasons to stay

1. I haven't finished listening to Adele's album 30, not all the way through. There's probably a lot of good songs I'd miss if I died now.
2. Peanut would have no one to bother when he's cold and tired and wants cuddles. None of the cats would. They need me, their mama, their favorite human, their very own screaming scratching-post.
3. I haven't eaten a Turkish delight that I fell in love with immediately. I've lied and said I enjoyed everyone I tried.
4. This gender thing is still confusing. I'd rather not die not knowing who I am.
5. My to-be-read pile has yet to get smaller, it instead has gotten higher. All those stories deserve to be read.
6. My story deserves to be read. But I need to tell it first.
7. Sunrises. Birds. spring summer fall winter. Trees. Sunsets. The moon.
8. Shrimp buffets. Are those a thing? I want them to be a thing.
9. Her. It's always for her. It will always be for her. Her.
10. Her: Molly. And her *Hamilton* playlists and her laughing when I'm crying over *Frozen 2* and her crying when I'm crying over *Spiderman: No Way Home*.

Robin Williams

a shotgun i pulled the trigger on left a gaping hole in my chest
and i wanted to fill it back up
with the splintered bones, torn skin, and rotted flesh
but you told me not to
said that it wouldn't ever heal that way and i should let it go
i thought you were crazy
but you told me "i've been here before"

and you showed me a scar across your chest
purple and smooth and healed
with the flattened bullet hanging around your neck
and you told me to trust you
and i did.

       —i'm alive and i won't say that you're the reason
         but you were the light my lost moth mind was drawn to

⊷⋯⊷

Robin Williams

I tell myself *this too will pass* and I pull the blanket up to my
chest
I tell myself *this too will pass* and I spoon chocolate chip cookie
dough ice cream into my mouth
I tell myself *this too will pass* and I sing the lyrics to what was
our song
I tell myself *this too will pass* and I write the love poems I
couldn't before
I tell myself *this too will pass* and it does

I'd read news stories
of people marrying themselves
and I'd think *how ridiculous.*

But what greater act of self-love is there
than declaring your devotion
to hold yourself accountable,
to love and cherish yourself,
to be your biggest supporter,
and to be your own source of happiness,
forever?

———•——➤❍❑·❑❍◄——•—

Robin Williams

I am not symmetrical.

My left eyebrow is arched, and my right is in a constant furrow
and my boobs are two different sizes, though that may be the tumor,
and I'm pretty sure my right leg is slightly longer than my left.

And maybe it's just the poet in me
but I think my imperfect symmetry
is a metaphor for something:

How life even in all its glory has no balance to it.

An acceptance email can be followed by five rejections.
A low engagement can be followed by forty-four shop sales.
My cats' happy purr can be followed by my other cats' stubborn attitude.

When I look at myself in the mirror
every morning after brushing my teeth
I do think to myself, "what a wonderful human being this is,"
and I know that my face is asymmetrical
and that maybe I'd change my eyebrows to match

but the rest of me will stay this way
and like all life

I can't be a mistake.

Robin Williams

Morning Affirmations

- I am enough.
- I am worthy of love.
- I deserve happiness, too.
- I will not hold on to the past, but in the case that I do, I will allow myself rest
    - for the hurting is tiring, and it isn't easy to remember
      that there was nothing I more could've done
      to make them stay.

———⧓⋅⧓———

Robin Williams

Self-Portrait of My Adolescent Insecurities
after Orion Carloto

The petite frame
I supposedly got from my mother
feels too small.
I want more.

My dark, full eyebrows
the middle schoolers pointed out
each morning under their breath.
Their snickers still haunt me.

These faded scars
from younger years and years of pain
I hope to never return to,
mark my skin their territory till I die.

The light blue eyes
and long dark lashes
I got from my father,
never an insecurity, but constantly
praised and noticed.
Why couldn't I see their beauty too?

Staring in the mirror,
cracked in pieces from the day I
"accidentally" knocked it over,
I connect the dots
and the picture appears:
Me—
I am still learning to love.

⊸⊷∞⋅∞⊶⊸

Robin Williams

I took a journey
many months ago to find a kind of gold
I could inject into my veins
so people would love me.
If I was worth something,
they'd stay.
If I was this shimmering star dust,
they'd find me beautiful.

I'm lying in the dark, now,
candlelight reflecting off
the dew drops on my skin,
warmth rippling through the grey,
everything shining in what only
can be described as a moment of peace.
A moment empty of everything
except for newfound love.

For I am home
from a journey
I never needed to take.
In this light, I am golden.

──────●──❮❯·❮❯──────●──
Robin Williams

Like the seasons I will change.
I will grow.
I will shed the things that no longer serve me.
And when it's time for me to rest, I will.

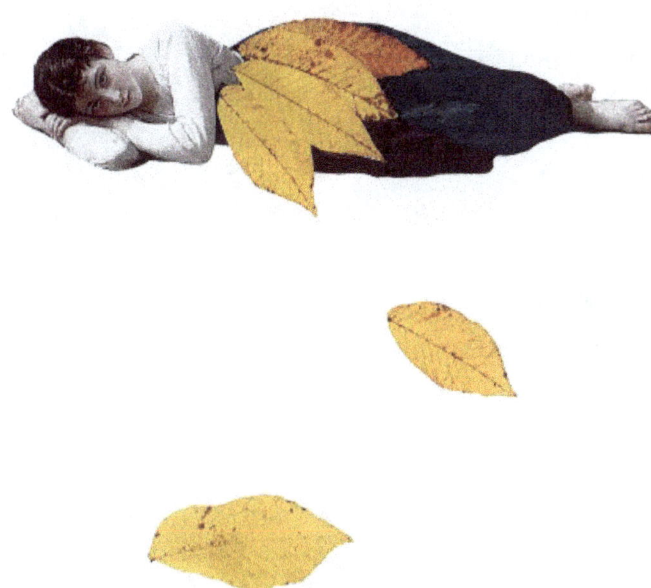

Robin Williams

I'm here, again,
in the space between okay
and falling apart,

a silent moment
where it's just my thoughts
and memories of you,
neither clawing at each other's throats.

It is calm and gentle,
like a breeze on a cool spring day,
and I know this space will pass.

It always does,
this longing.

Its shouts will fade away,
and I will be okay.

———⊃⊂⊂·⊃⊂⊂———

Robin Williams

in time,
this winter will pass
and i won't hold your cold hands in mine.

spring will bring flowers
and dewdrops will rest on my eyelashes
instead of freezing to my cheeks.

love will be soft
like butterfly wings
and i will feel warmth once again.

i will smile once again.

Robin Williams

Asexual

Also called: "haven't met the right person yet," "you'll change your mind," "broken"

1.1 Overview

I. asexual is the lack of sexual attraction to others

II. asexual is my mother crying at an Arby's because i refuse to have kids

III. asexual is your gynecologist asking if you're sexually active at every appointment when the notes specifically say "no. not once. never."

1.2 Symptoms

I. you may experience discomfort when your friends talk about how many guys they've slept with

II. you may experience first dates going well and seconds and thirds and a text at 3am reading "i don't think i can do this, being with an ace. sorry."

III. you may experience late nights on cold tiled floors in dimly lit bathrooms crying because how could anybody love you?

1.3 Treatments

I. treatment depends on the individual's willingness to accept that there are no treatments

II. there is nothing

III. wrong

IV. with

V. you

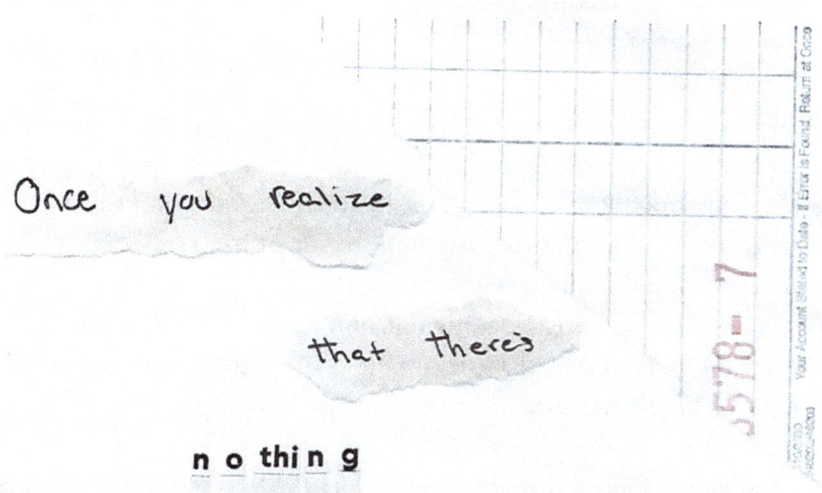

Once you realize

that there's

n o thi n g

wrong with you,

you become

u n st op pa b le

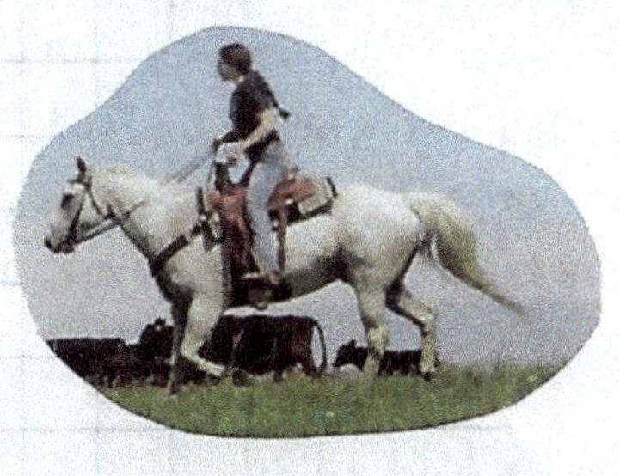

Robin Williams

If you were to ask me
Do you regret anything?
I would tell you
No.

If we are speaking about regret from the events that unfolded in the hospital room during my junior year of high school, the answer would be no, I regret nothing.
The truth was going to come out one way or another, one day before I died, and it just so happened to be between the breath of *do I have to answer that question* and silence.

An endless silence, I might add, at least it felt endless. It felt like time had decided to stop and let me mellow in the mess I had just begun to create, as it always does. Time is never on our side. Even after the phone call with my mother, her sobbing on the other line, the police came and took her boy, time did not slow down for answers, it did not speed up for it all to be over like we asked.

Yes, we. We all asked for it to end.

Though each plea was different for different people.
I pleaded for the world to fall off its axis and roll around the immense space of darkness and stars, and for my stomach to stop shouting for ham and cheese sandwiches from the hospital cafe, and for my crying to be more silent and calmer and not crashing like a waterfall over a one man boat.
You'd have to ask the others what their pleas were for, though bring tissues and thick skin, for all the crying and yelling you'd be bound to endure.

It's a touchy subject, sexual assault is.

————————

Robin Williams

The days now are shorter
and the list of things I feel guilty about is too.

That evening where I apologized to you
still sits on the tip of my tongue,
an apology I wish I could take back and forget about

because the reaction of being thanked for forgiving you
          stings,
a throbbing pain.

I didn't need to apologize,
I hadn't done anything but fear for my life
in the fist of mother nature.

You   ruined
your own   life
when you laid your hands   on me

I am only ashamed that it took me so long to realize this.
But maybe if I had known I didn't need to apologize,
if the reaction wasn't the reaction it had been,
I might have realized sooner.

——————⊷⊶∙⊷⊶——————

Robin Williams

i lit a candle to renounce my faith

to renounce
the sunday mornings / the preaching about our loss of freedom / the filing cabinet filled with pages upon pages telling me i'm a sin / the pastor who looked me in the eye and told me suicide was selfish / the class in which she told me because my friend ruined god's creation, he was going to hell / the jesus who died for my mistakes but not that one and not that one either / the man who dressed as our saint nicholas / the man who went to facebook to make islamophobic posts / the way my father tells me god has a plan / the way my mother pretends i still believe / the person i used to be

devoted and scared.
to the person i am now
content and free

Robin Williams

I don't ever have to forgive you.

Robin Williams

I tend to hyperfocus on one thing,
or one cluster of things,
until I lose interest.

Or in the case of our brokenness,
inspiration.

I've hyper focused on
losing the title of an "us"
for well over a year now,

the wells of inspiration have dried up,
and everything I said once
I've begun to say again.

While some may see this as the death of a poet,
the lifeline we cling onto snipped,
I see it as my healing,

my recovery.

I have loved you for a lifetime
and I know I always will,
but this time I am loving myself,

I am letting you go
and holding on to me.

———⊷⧓·⧓⊶———

Robin Williams

Things I Know Now That I Wish I Knew Then

1. Healing isn't linear.
2. It's okay to still grieve the love I lost.
3. It's going to hurt for a little while.
4. It wasn't my fault, and it wasn't theirs. Sometimes love just isn't meant to last.
5. I don't need permission to love who I want to love.

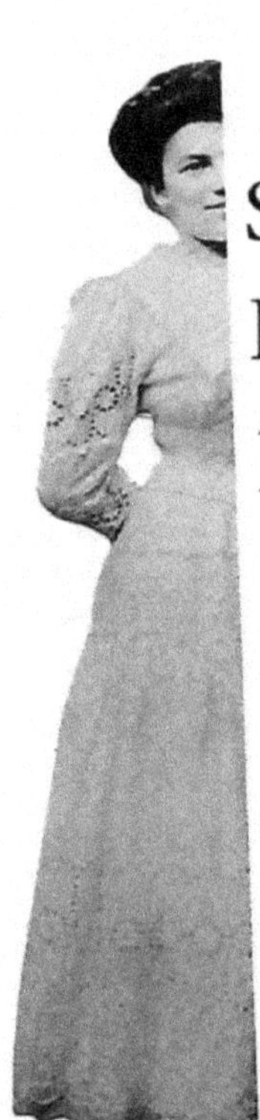

SELF-
REFLECTION

HIDES UNDER

A BANDAID

I'M TOO

AFRAID TO

RIP OFF

I had promised to work on myself,
to calm my tongue,
to put my impulsivity on a leash,
and to cool the temper seething inside me.

But to do that means to confess
in a blank paint peeling booth,
to look myself in the eyes
and admit my wrongs aloud.

In each drop of ink,
it is easier to blame you,
to make my soul as pure as the white empty page,
than it is to tarnish the image I have of myself.

The first step to my apology lies in waiting
until I peel the beige band-aid off
and I admit I am afraid
of what I've hidden underneath my skin.

But I want to mean it
when I tell you I'm sorry
and so, for you...

Robin Williams

I talk to you about money/the empty space between the folds of
my wallet/the red numbers against clean white on my bank
statements/the memories of having no power/no hot water/in
the middle of winter/with snow on the ground//
You talk to me about money/the way it makes you feel helpless
when you hold nothing between your fingers/the urge to just
pick up any job if it means one less bill plaguing your mind/and I
listen to you, only partly//
With my eyes half rolled/and my temper half controlled/and my
annoyance half down//
Because I can talk/complain/worry/about the lack of necessities
in my life/but if you/or other/talk/complain/worry/about the
lack of/I grow impatient with the subject/waiting for its
change//
Because my toxic trait/is wanting people to care/about me/but I
don't want to care/about them/despite my want *to* care/I can't

This Poem Is Titled   HYPOCRISY

An apology letter pt.2

Dear me,

I know the breakup nearly killed you. I know you wouldn't dare tell a soul, at least not theirs, for fear of making them feel guilty. I know you told your family at least once, during that week of endless begging at ungodly hours in the morning, between ugly crying and miserable silence, while you talked to a stranger on the other line. He felt like a stranger, completely absent from the moment. Couldn't blame him, though. You were pretty embarrassing.

But I need you to forgive yourself for it. I need you to knock it off, feeling guilty about the way you acted, holding regret inside of you. I need you to let it all go. I can't heal with you continuously grasping for those memories like your life ended at that very hour. You still have a life; I'm trying to live that life. So for god's sake, please, forgive yourself.

And while we're still on the topic of the things that dragged you through hell, I need to remind you that anger will get you nowhere.

Correction: it will get you some places, but I mean mentally, you're going nowhere. It's like you're sitting at a gas station, in the middle of some dirt-road county, having an existential crisis because you're out of gas and stuck there. And no, I am not saying you need to forgive him, I don't want you to forgive him. But I do want you to realize that you've got gas to fill your car with, you can leave now, if you would just look around you. As soon as you're ready to stop being so angry, you can take a big

Robin Williams

breath, and move forward. You can still have your moments, just remember who you're talking to, and ask yourself if they're the ones who deserve your lashings.

You have a lot of self-growth to do, and I will admit I had my back turned from you. I wasn't very helpful till after everything crumbled down, and I'm sorry for that, for not being there for you to tell you some things weren't your fault. But I am here, now, and together maybe we can work on untangling some knots.

It'll take some time   but doesn't everything?

Best,
Robin

Things to Note:

"in this dimension i...," was first published with *The Sapphic Printing Press.*
"Murky Waters," was first published with *Moss Puppy Magazine.*
"Asexual," was first published with *Blackbird Publishing.*
"Driftwood," was first published with *Free Verse Revolution.*
"A portrait...," was first published with *Warning Lines Magazine.*

"the need to survive lit a fire in me" was written after Rupi Kaur's poem of the same name.
"i opened a fortune cookie one afternoon and it said something to the effect of, 'do what you love to do,' was written after Parker Lee's poem of the same name.
"THINGS YOU ARE NOT ALLOWED TO LOOK AT" was written after Skyler Saunders' poem of the same name.
"Things that terrify me, and more," was written after Shreya's (scorpionbeds) poem of the same name.
"Self-Portrait of My Adolescent Insecurities" was written after Orion Carlotto's poem of the same name.

The blackout poem *"Mothertongue"* was made using the prose piece *"Rabbits Love Roadkill"*, first published in *Scars of Apollo.*

The poem title *"stay alive, that would be enough"* is a line from the musical *Hamilton.*

The lines *"That's not loving someone. I know."* and *"If [they] asked me again, I think I would say..."* are from the *Little Women* (2019) movie.

Author, short film director, spoken word album producer, femme who makes god quiver... there is nothing Robin Williams, a queer poet from Pennsylvania, can't do. They've written the chapbook GIRL., published with Querencia Press, and wild honey, self-published, and have had previous publications in the Horizon Literary Magazine, Moss Puppy magazine, Warning Lines magazine, Free Verse Revolution magazine, and many more. When not tormenting the patriarchy, Robin can be found watching Little Women for the four-hundredth time or spending time outdoors with her family of eight cats.

Instagram: @paperbackfern
Website: www.greenferncoven.com